The Letters Unsent

We bit our tongues
to hold on to the pearls of words
every single pearl to never leave the oyster,
a necklace choked in our throats forever.

We hid these pearls,
within letters folded over and over
each fold sealed with the burnt oils,
that one day used to shine our faces and smiles.

And we keep these letters unsent,
protected by nightmares in our mind cabinets
trained our soul to live as cowards,
courage left as time grew older and wiser.

But one day if we still crave that lost wealth,
I place the key to these hidden cabinets
under the rugs for when we will sleep on the floor,
just too poor to find warmth on a bed.

Sunlight Love

The clouds are carpets
A hummingbird the hymn
Lakes, the jittery cajolers
And I rise as the welcome flower.

So lucky we are
When spreads across a sheet of laden gold
Jealous palaces have never worn such robes
When it's noon and this flower grows.

It runs today into my mouth
and my tongue tastes immortality
this flower's eyes are closed
But burnt a tear held below.

You the fire of candles in lonely nights
You the chariot of dreams in strides
You the symbol of everlasting love in tribes
You are this flower heart's cry of joy.

The Mirrors Stopped Reflecting

Broken their forbidden oaths
to serve endlessly the human folks,
closed them their crystal eyes
to reflect again our cloudy minds.

Turned their gray backs
to bury their face in the silent walls,
drunk them all our wine
to ease the suffering, we caused in their life.

Unheard the evils we said
unseen the evils we showed,
they who get tired without a step
with reflections of our cursed souls.

Sink so they today, their liquid heart
never beat to see the blood poured on our arms,
wipe them their lightning memory
to forget the misery, time reflects.

Value of a Tear

Maybe my tears and eyelids
play a game of see-saw
either the tears fall for the heavy memories
or the eyelids close for my dreams.

Maybe put my tear in your eye
To know about the fire
which makes these tears drop
so, I can come out of the fire unburnt.

Maybe our tears are just
little travelers that board our bus
several leave at the small stops in between
Some pay the full price to shine where we belong.

Voices of the Jungle

when the wind blows across the jungle
leaves hustle on the twigs which bustle,

the sunshine streams through pores of thickets
grass gleams on the dew teams,

the woody musky smell rises in the air
bees swarm on the floret farm,

deer and bears give their heads a twirl
the tiger cubs walk, and the turtles talk,

fiery fast tails of monkeys and fishes
peacock dance in grace while eagles soar in the race,

little rain drops while the sun glistens
insect sounds below the lights of firefly rounds,

moon shines and the stars twinkle
voices of the jungle going on.

With Your Face in My Eyes

With your face in my eyes
I cry a tear
And the moon just stares
never it looked so beautiful even over the ocean.

the waves which never stop
Now are shy
From a tear with your face in my eyes
never have they seen a single drop so powerful.

And now even death is afraid
to close my eyes
Where sits your face
Not yet has she seen a death so beautiful.

*5*4 = 20*

Read it over and over
Till dusk to dawn
Never knew it meant
Fingers of my palms crossed in yours.

Does it mean
All that I read
All that I worked on
Were mysteries to find you in my arms.

I just want to say
I still have not been in
One class forever in my life
But I don't mind failing this time.

The Noble Soul of a Candle

I have seen people around candles
melting below the fiery flame
drops of tears are poured
cut from a noble sword within.

emerging from the price of peace
a noble soul surrounds
when wrapped around by hands
She wears a bright golden cloak around.

So, while the people huddle back
to their busy dark lives
a noble soul flickers still within
Healing the forever cuts of their eyes.

Lines

These single lines
What do you say?
I hear you started from a point
Where everyone laughed an honest smile

These single lines
Then what happened?
What made you choose to fly
In a ride that takes you to the stars in the sky

These single lines
Don't you see?
You run so fast and hard
But curves are eventually the destiny

These single lines
Don't you know?
It's okay for some to be slow
Still smiling away the pointless silliness below

Live Like Birds

Earliest to wake
fastest to sleep
over our heads
a beautiful beep.

A swift head
a curved thick beak
hunting for food
protecting the weak.

On a cold day
giving glimpses of hope
on a windy day
they swing and elope.

Colors of rainbow
finer than the works of Picasso
feathers shining light
faster than the fingers of Django.

See the birds fly over
follow how they live
listen they are a happy chirp
feel they have much to give.

My Poetry Is Wandering Far, Far Away

Resting just a little too long
Between the valleys in my head
She hears a wind through my hair
And seeks to fly where my eyes end.

Not heeding anymore, the red stop signs
and away from the beaches of sandy feet
She seeks a dance where the sun kisses the sea
to find pleasure of dreams without a sleep.

Every night now, I feel her words drift away
Like the smell of boiling coffee that never waits
The wine I drink not drowsy to make her rest
instead makes my poetry wander far, far away.

I ask her what she finds
so far from her birthplace at the horizon
just other poems written by some, and she smiles
who wish to wander far, far away.

Is There a Pure Heart?

I have imagined a heart
a heart so pure,
that has made friends
with teardrops and laughter both.

Whenever this heart now
finds a little home to rest,
the eyes bring out the curtains
And the cheeks widen across as carpets.

A Little Push

A little push
Can turn the wheel
Draw water from the ground beneath.

A little push
Can flip a held coin
Turn around the tailing destinies.

A little push
Can open the held bird
Fly to the end of the skies.

A little push
Can make the tired
Still hold onto the rope ends.

A little push
Can bring us close
Turn this push to a love pull.

Do the Words Cry Also?

Seen people break
but do words feel sad
When unheard and left back.

When they are thrown
uncared, unthought
unused left away in the dark.

In the night you can see them
slip off the pages
tear into letters to leave any meaning.

How long will they survive
cut themselves silently one day
with the pencil that brought them alive.

I just know that
when the words will bleed
the world will remain silent for quite a while.

Diving in a Teardrop of a Silent Face

I have dived in the ocean, river and lake
But today I took a leap
To a depth no one has ever reached

I saw a silent face
And a teardrop on shivering cheeks
Making no sound surrounded by the air around.

I could not have just walked by
So decided to stay and say
Could I hold you in the depths of a cry

In these depths lies no life
Just some echoes survive
Of promises unkept and killed by time.

How long could I stay here
I knew my breath just had a few more sighs
And so, I did what I could

Stayed inside this tear
Till my last breath remained
And came out to see a bunch of tears crying

But with a smile on the silent face.

A Rude Day

I decided today
I will not smile at any passerby
Not hold the door for a single soul
Utter no thanks to the kind folks.

The day went by
my arrogance reached the sky
I broke every heart I could find
growing the list of tragedy cries.

The evening came quite too soon
So happy was I being so rude
I told the mounting guilt too
This was the day of the rude.

Then came the time to sleep
my eyes still seeking more to be rude
but I only found a mirror and realized
this rude day ends being rude to my soul too.

The Face Behind the Mirror

Have you seen the face
Behind the mirror
With silent stares morning and night.

That face must be lonely
Never I have seen it with friends
Never a cup of wine in its hands.

Maybe the face is tired
From watching me with my friends
Pouring a smile till the night ends.

So today I smile for that face
Make it feel a part of my soul
For somehow I feel that might complete me.

When Did I See My Poetry Happy

I saw my poetry
Lonesome and worried
When asked to fight another one,
I saw my poetry
Happiest has it been
When asked to find another one.

Whispers Between the Sun and the Moon

The sun asked the moon
I know your love for the Earth
but why seek my cover during the day?
Moon said I like the silent dreams
unworthy are their talks during the day.

I will burn them said the flaring sun
to which the moon cried
Spare their talks oh sun,
for your fire will burn the ones
who still sing the kind whispers each night.

Who are they?
asked the surprised sun.
And the moon smiled
the ones who sleep under my light
waiting for you to pull the covers of the night.

Shadows of Sun's Tears

The sun woke
With eyes so hopeless
Deep cuts of red blood stains,

Like a dimming oil lamp
He stood in the skies
Even the flowers didn't notice his shine.

Such a lonesome ball
No one to hold and ask
Until mother clouds held him in her arms,

And fed him the pure milk they hold
While making countless cloud shapes
singing the nursery rhymes in the sky.

But he burst the boiled anger in the skies
While the world lived unaware
In the shadows of the sun's tears.

How Can You Not Fall in Love?

How can you not fall in love
With someone who shows their soul?
Maybe the question is
Do you not love yourself?
Or worse, have you forgotten who you are?

Just Don't Rub Your Eyes Away

Don't rub away your eyes
Where lie oceans I sail
For these waves you will create
Shipwrecks are the final fate

These tearful sad rubs
Will sink me away
To an old cold memory
Lying far from the sunlight where we played.

Don't you remember my first sail
From the shores unknown
Scouting corners of your eye waters till the night
Where below the stars I met a mermaid's soul

So even if I caused you pain
Shout out your anger rage
This boat has lasted to sail below thunder clouds
Close its sail if the winds blow out.

But if you do need to cry
Give me a chance to see the sun once more
Forgive me to take a little eyelid as a raft
Even if this love ship sinks, my memory on it may float.

The Pressure on Words

I hear the voice
And the pressure on the few words
Squeezed tight like a spring
Like a forest waterfall never heard.

Why hide your voice
Why bury the living touch of your soul
Let it flow today
Let it release like the volcano.

Have you not tasted yet
The best coffee grown after a lava flow.

Silence Plays a Mystical Game

Sometimes in between
The sounds of words
Silence plays a mystical game.

We start listening to the silence
Start believing when she is next to us
and find comfort with who we are silent around.

Such a spell without chants
The game of silence where none is defeated
For silence is mystical after all.

A Melted Love

Me and you
Were ice in bourbon
Passionately drunk we started
But once we melted
Our fire doused forever.

Sometimes Poetry Takes Time

I have walked on the streets
And felt these times
Connected where were we
As if we seek the same destiny.

But I did not hear a voice
Or a laugh
Nor a rope that tied all our hands
Neither we had the same train stop.

Nothing but poetry stood with us
But she took her dear time
It was not till my watch tired
I saw her hold our hands.

Sometimes poetry does take time
To show her old silver smile
For when she sweetly does
Our laughs won't learn to be quiet.

A Moment Before a Smile Is to Be Seen

This boat is slow, but the harbor is close
I am the boat, the water and the peddler
everything moves and there is no anchor
There is no stop as the souls are filling this crater.

And in the rush, I will just remember this breeze
which brought a laugh before I crossed the crease
So just before the smile will melt away
The crew holds warm covers before landing on the bay.

Reliving these moments at this time later
Brings forth a tear
which still leaks from the old crater
From a moment before a smile is to be seen.

If Her Each Hair Were a Wish

If her each hair were a wish
Won't I be twisting destiny
Smelling the world of fantasies
Pulling till luck itself needed remedy.

If her each hair were a wish
Every day will be a lamp rub
Following along each wish fountain
To drown every night where the luck ended.

Stillness of Water

This water which shows
Reflections of my sunlit face
spreads my smile a little more
in the depths untouched,
So far, I don't know
if now smiles the water or me anymore.

Do not now shake this water
For I don't want to lose this smile
Neither am I the fish
Nor the sunlight has in the depths shined.
All that will be left is the red wine
A lost smile will bleed the stillness of my mind.

Reflections of a Poem

Do poems remember
When they were born
And rose with their first yawn

They saw their house
Where they learned to play
Made friends with words on the porch I lay.

They learnt to know the village
And the way back to their house
Her soulful steps making a route for life.

She grew from words to a poem,
her childlike jumps settled
deciding who would finally frame her.

But does she still remember
This old poet who got her to life
I see engraved my name in the backyard of her house.

She Always Understood Me

I wrote and wrote
Each word a breath to give her
Yet she never felt the warmth
From the fire these word coals let off.

But the day she saw me drowning
She came like a bubble in the sea
And my shivers she wiped away
From the heat her touch steamed.

I gave her all the poetry
But she was a poem herself
So even if I could not understand her
She always understood me.

Zero and Infinity

I never understood zero
Nor did I grasp infinity
But the day I started writing poetry
I started making an imaginary friend daily.

Now the day I don't write
The absence of my imaginary friend haunts me
And the day I write, I wish
another imaginary friend's smile.

Now I know why
They made zero and infinity.

Behind the Curtain

Behind the curtain
The words I seek
What do they say to me?

As the sun rises
I see their shadows play on the wall
Which I draw on pages till he falls.

And then the night fills in
These playful shadows
To finish the left shapes in my sleep.

Behind the curtain
The words know it all
Asking the sun and the night to just play along.

A Poem That Ends Before It Begins

There is a poem
Where tomorrow is thought
Before today is lived

Where the color of night wine is set
Before the sun dips
sunsets form before sunrise awakens the seas.

It is a poem
where answers are written
And the worried questions run behind

A poem that
Shows water to form the thirst
Fruits are seen before the bees flirt.

A poem where
Children are made
From the adults we live,

I know there is this poem
For I am awake
But it sounds like sleeping in a dream.

A Repeating Voice

Heard this voice
A slight kiss
over the road you move?

I am here
and so are you
Why not we be two?

A voice heard from the leaf
Keychain, soil heaps
Water drops or shoes

Give me a breath
and I will give you
a smile to hold onto.

A Voice now rattles
from another rail in the train
lean and grip me today

This little kiss
From these voices
Like those forever repeating waves.

An Evening Eighth Note

The cup lies on the side
my fingers on this old paper
I look at the wall in the front
Drinking the sounds in the sun.

Oh, this stillness of air
My mind smells the coffee and gaffs
It's not time to still rest
Says my mind with a jumping heart.

My mind scolds you forgot again
We listen now to this note missed
As we begin our hunt in the midnight hour
To hear what the eighth note sings.

Day passing baton to her night partner
As the road outside curls in slumber
leaves of trees have started snoring
When the eighth note wakes from its dreaming.

The floor is happy to have felt many feet
But the walls complain about the windy slaps
The joyous oranges have formed their standup
And the alone sofa harps its big bass.

Such is the loud silence of the eighth note,
It needs the breath of our hearts to ring
So, I the record-keeper take another sip of coffee
To note tales before begins the morning crass.

When Smiles Combine

A smile can hold a drop
but two can save it
for the dry day of thirst,

A smile can reflect the sun
but two can keep the light
When the dark night has rust.

A smile can feel the dream
but two can let it echo between
for when the hopeless sleep swings by,

A smile might erode away,
but two can protect the memories
of these beautiful mornings that fly.

Lucky Times

Some lucky times
I am given a few friends
The other lucky times
There are endless poems.

With both I speak
With both I hear
One shows me to live
One shows me not to give up

One sets the campfire
One drinks the glass
With both there are endless desires
To let the night to last

But they say time doesn't stop
Lucky times beaten by the clock
Friends they wander too far
poems remain enclosed within walls.

A Laugh Torn in Your Voice

I listen to your voice
As we talk fast and slow
But like a river opens to the sunlight
A laugh tears open your voice flows

I hang on to these tears
Keep searching for a few more
Even throw stones of my funny faces
To ripple more in your voiced notes.

So just keep your torn river still flowing
Don't bring out yet the mouth tapes
If we were meant to be
Our kiss will calm these laughter waves

Unequal Steps

The steps that were
once so straight
now suddenly seem so staggered.

Feet that could once
walk on rocky hills
now fear the slips over paved roads.

The walk
even sand couldn't topple
has been swept away by the sea.

Where did we part?
when was the last time
These unequal steps were together.

A Buried Poetry

Don't keep the poetry within you
Buried down so deep in the well
That one day when you pull on the rope
It chokes the poetry while climbing for a breath.

A Lemon Sea

I imagine a sea
Where grow lemon trees with lemon leaves
Floating over roots with lemons beneath,

Here the sun does not wait till the edge of sea
But rises in between
from the morning lemon squeeze,

And when it gets a little hot
Poured are little lemon rains from lemon clouds
With lemon lights that shine birds with lemon beaks.

Here fishes sip the lemon water to sleep
flat lemon flowers attract owls with lemon eyes
As lemon breeze sways over chunks of lemon ice,

And finally at night
come together the left lemon seeds to form a moon
greeting lemon lovers who drink the lemon juice.

Knock of Words

Have the words ever knocked on your door
And asked to paste them on a page
giving a curious stare like the Mona Lisa
And you forever wonder what they wanted to say

Is There a Bad Time for Poetry?

I asked the poetry
Is there a time
She does not like the reading eye
Or the hand that writes?

The poetry laughed
Said oh you foolish boy
Will the land ever not let you sit
Or the sky not let you fly?

Just remember there is a time to lay and dream
And another to stand and fly in the sky.

If Each Drop Were a Word

If each drop were a word
Will there still be a sea
Through which sunrise and sunsets will find a way
To wake or bring the world to sleep?

And will it ever rain
Or will there be sadness of words on cheeks?
I am just sure that the mirages would still exist
Read on hopeless days by wine lovers of the street.

Sitting Around a Table

The people came and sat
The glasses were laid
Forks kept on hitting the plates
As the cherries on the cakes gave way.

The chatter goes in and out
As lights go bright and dim
Everyone starts to converse
Yet the windows keep calling your name.

So, you take a look outside
World asking for a bite of you
will you surrender away as the world shouts
Is your soul just worth a cherry or two?

A Poetic Maze

Sometimes it's confusing
Should I rhyme
Should each tide be the same

Sometimes it's clear
The path is left right left
Every thought hits the target straight.

Sometimes it's both
equal tides reflect differently the sunlight
Each clear thought, the brain wanders off path.

But the fun lies
When it is neither clear nor confusing
When the word tides rise without our knowing.

Clap, Just Clap

I have seen
people staring in the air
Unaware their breath too flies there

Their chest quietly moves
Eyes still, nothing left to see
Thoughts paralyzed like the far burning mirages.

Tell me you are alive in your heart
Tell me you have an ask
You made it, hug this breath you released today

Clap, let's celebrate this victory together.

As I Play Just for Those Forgotten Moments of Smile

In the night I pluck some notes
being no good in rhythm or melody

these notes so out of beat or tune
but still resonate those forgotten moments of smile.

Maybe they parallel my heartbeat
the rainbow spring toy held at both hands

emotions break these walls around
I swim in torrents, climb hills while I am here but am not here.

What I could do with this rusty old guitar
and my spirit seeks salvation in this night with the owl

I see faces, I see dreams
I seek chaos with a divine rhythm

As I play just for those forgotten moments of smile.

Chairs Waiting for a Warmth

Like a home with no lights
are a few empty seats
hearts that beat on legs paralyzed.

Look at a few closely today
don't they ask you to sit on them
To have seconds away from a lonely life

So, I sit on this seat
in between the walkers and runners
and the seat wears me like covers of a warm bed

Finally, some sleep to find her cold tired shoulders.

A River Decided to Change Her Flow

All these rivers
Fall into the sea
To join their friends
cutting the rocks, watering the trees.

But I know of a river
With a lot of fishes that leap
That is still searching
Cutting, watering still flowing with the breeze.

The fishes inside don't know
Where the river will end
They have been through forests
Escaping the nets of the fishermen.

Touched by everyone
The river has not found its home
the rains pour if she is tired and shallow
voices sing of the hundred paths it follows.

The Black Window Between Stations

the bright light fades
and we again stare at the black window
reflecting with gray boundaries

the black window knows it all
sees tears that have stopped
hearing minds in the deaf crowd.

Here live dreams and fights
the black window holds drinks of the night
intoxicating little glints in our eyes

glints that push the shrouds off
melt the gray boundaries
dare us to see beyond the forbidden lines.

The bright light shines
and we stare at a dam instead,
but the dreams have been sown in the melt.

A Mermaid's Beauty

This beauty is unable to find
reflections of her face
For the jealous fishes inside
ripple the water into waves.
Oh fishermen, cast down your nets
Catch a thousand fishes
When the last fish is caught
You may release the mermaid.

www.ingramcontent.com/pod-product-compliance
Lightning Source LLC
Chambersburg PA
CBHW072037060426
42449CB00010BA/2307